THE FILIPINO NURSE IN AMERICA

A glimpse into our Filipino nurses' life, passion, and journey of coming to America. Short Stories.

BINIBINI MINNERVA

The Filipino Nurse
Copyright © 2022 by Binibini Minnerva

ISBN: Paperback:978-1962204-36-1
ISBN: Hardcover:978-1962204-37-8

Dedication

Thank you to a God that cannot be seen by the naked eye yet felt by us every day. You created nurses so humanity can feel your love and care. Thank you, Jesus, for dying on the cross and sending nurses along the way.

Everyone has the chance to make an impact on the lives of many people. To the nurses who willingly shared their journey, thank you for the inspiring stories.

To my nursing colleagues, may the power be with you as you give care to humanity. You turn fear, pain, and anxiety, to name a few, into something bearable because of your presence. For some patients, you are the gentle presence who will provide them the care they need as they go through the most vulnerable phase of sickness. To some, you are there to cheer for them and celebrate with them as they bring life into this world in the form of a newborn baby. To others, you are the eyes that are needed to bring data together. The work of your hand is countless. What will the world be without a nurse?

To our fallen nurses who died of COVID while caring for others, I hope we will have more nurses like you. Nurses who care. Nurses who serve in times of uncertainty so others can get well.

To Daddy, you got to enjoy heaven early. We surely miss you, but no eye has seen nor ear has heard what you are enjoying there. Thank you for your love. Thank you for being a dedicated teacher and father.

Contents

THE NURSES

Foreword

From the first time I met Mimie thirty four years ago, I knew that she would be a rockstar in the nursing field. There was something about her effortlessness with which she styled her tresses and how her curls chose to flow. Her smile was sweet and full of warmth and kindness. Her self-confidence exhibited impressive cognitive ability and knowledge, yet she was humble. Her dreams and aspirations were vast, limitless, and awe-inspiring. Starting a life in America was one of the precious dreams that we shared together.

The journey of pursuing life in America was exceptionally challenging .The agony of leaving my family behind was the most heartbreaking knowing there was no turning back. The process of making my dream a reality was nothing short of a roller coaster. I had to believe in myself that I could make it through and failure was never an option. I had devoted the last eighteen years of my nursing career in Critical Care. Regrettably, my passion for ICU nursing came to an abrupt halt after my grueling battle with cancer .I beam with pride and joy that I had the inimitable chance to serve and care for all of my patients in that fleeting amount of time. I am hopeful in prayer that I was able to make a difference in their invaluable lives. I am forever blessed and grateful.

Binibining Minnerva, your quest and fulfillment for higher education degrees in Masters in Nursing, Nurse Practitioner, and Doctorate in Family Nurse Practitioner came nothing as a surprise. Your dedication and commitment to healthcare is immeasurable.
You are a blessing to everyone around you. You touch people's loves more than you know. You have a beautiful mind and soul. I am very happy, proud and beyond pleased of your great achievements and our special bond of friendship. With so much

love and gratitude, I thank you, our dearest America for making our dreams come true.

May you be inspired by all these nurses' captivating stories and experiences of selfless love and care for humanity. May your spirits be lifted by these nurses' courage, compassion, bravery, sacrifice ,hard work, resilience, perseverance, and determination. May this amazing book bring a smile to your heart knowing that you have nurses to count on both blissful and arduous times of your existence.

To all the Filipino nurses and nurses around the world, may we never waiver. May we continue to do good, be righteous ,and kind. May God's guidance and blessings be always upon us. Thank you so much for sharing your lives to all. Mabuhay tayong lahat!

Ivy Tan Rombaoa
BSN,RN,CCRN (Inactive status)

Foreword

The United States has long been a popular destination for Filipino nurses due to its competitive wages and excellent working conditions. Financial need is the driving force of a Filipino nurse to migrate, but not all. Fortunately, in most cases, the dream of a greener pasture comes to fruition. That is with a lot of hard work and sacrifices. Filipino registered nurses, myself included, believe in the worth and dignity of each human being and recognizes the primary responsibility to preserve health at all cost. If life is lost, you cannot take it back. It is a job that mistakes cannot be made. Nurses' values are Love of God, Family and Country, Quality Care, Excellence, Integrity, Honesty, and more. In summation, to me, it is a very noble profession, and I wore the nurses' cap and pin with pride. "Sink or swim," as the saying goes, but because of the resiliency of the Filipino nurses, they emerged. The stories shared in this book are meant to inspire others, and may we learn valuable lessons. God bless us all.

Macbeth Torno
Retired RN
PNAAZ President (2008-2010)

Preface

When you go to a medical place, you see nurses everywhere. You can find a Filipino nurse among the many faces who will greet you. There are many Filipino nurses in the United States; if we are to compare other nurses who migrated to the United States, Filipino nurses comprise the largest group. Many of us dream of coming to America. For so many of us, being here fulfills that American dream.

The concept for this book came about when I met one Filipino nurse. She had just arrived a few months back when I met her. Her story of struggle and triumph inspired me, and I thought there must be others who could tell their stories and inspire others.

This project is born out of love for the nursing profession and for our Filipino nurses. The stories that you are about to read are a glimpse into the lives of our Filipino nurses who risked their future, left their families behind and all the familiar things in the hope of a better future.

The stories were gathered through face-to-face interviews over a meal (which most Filipinos love to do-eating), email correspondence, and telephone calls.

"Almost 16 percent of the nurses in the United States are immigrants, and nearly a third of those - the largest share - are Filipinos."

The New York Times

Almendral , A. (2020, June 22). On Pandemic's Front Lines, Nurses From Half a World Away. *The New York Times.* https://www.nytimes.com/2020/04/20/world/asia/coronavirusphilippinesnurses.html

CHAPTER ONE

I BECAME A NURSE BECAUSE OF THE KINDNESS OF MY RELATIVE

RIZZA D. BACOLOD

Rizza, as she is fondly called, is one of the nurses everyone notices with a big smile and a big heart. Here is her story:

My Journey of Becoming a Nurse

Growing up, my parents' meager income as a teacher and factory worker was not enough to give me and my five siblings the luxury of new clothes, toys, shoes, or even books.

The only time we got this stuff was when our cousins would give their used ones to us, our aunt would sponsor our dress if we got an award, or we were included in the honor's list. But despite this, we never felt how underprivileged we were. We learned to appreciate everything we had at a very young age.

At seven years of age, having a devoted Catholic grandma, I was in the church with her every Saturday afternoon as a member of the Legion of Mary, praying the rosary while my siblings and other kids my age were at home playing.

I remember my first teaching experience was at the age of 10, during the Flores de Mayo. To me, my faith and devotion to Mama Mary are my lifeline.

Life became tougher for my family when my father passed away when I graduated from high school. Having my mother support her six children alone, she exhausted all the options, including asking her distant relative for a scholarship for me.

God is always good, as He introduced me to a very kind and generous family who supported all my college education without asking anything in return except to finish my nursing degree and help my mother send my siblings to school after I graduated. I can proudly say two of my siblings are registered nurses, a teacher, marketing and finance, and my only brother as a certified mechanical engineer.

Academic Achievements

I graduated Cum Laude in 1993 with a Bachelor of Science in Nursing at Colegio de San Agustin-Bacolod.

In Choosing Nursing

It was the situation I was in, the preference of my sponsor for me to take up Nursing instead of teaching and to help my family. I can say it's an economic reason why I chose nursing, but it was my passion for being a nurse that I stayed in this profession.

Working As A Nurse in the Philippines

I graduated in 1993. While I was waiting for the result of the Board Exam, I worked as an office assistant in the review center for the local boards and CGFNS (Commission on Graduates Of Foreign Nursing Schools) in Bacolod City.

I went to Manila, looked for a job, and experienced the hard life in the big city because of the high cost of living. In 1995, I ended up working at Pocket Bell (a paging service company), first as an operator and then as a customer service representative. That became my first exposure to the corporate world.

I enjoyed my work in Pocket Bell as it is parallel to taking care of patients and training you on how to have a good customer service experience.

By 1996, I started working as a nurse. I worked as a private nurse to a Filipina actress. I got free board and lodging and sent my financial assistance to my mom. At the same time, I worked at Jose Viray Memorial Hospital in the Makati area.

Seeking For a Greener Pasture

In 2000, I married my husband Ted in a civil ceremony. Though already married, I worked in Singapore for five years to support my siblings, who were in college. I loved and enjoyed working in Singapore and learned the importance of discipline and hard work.

In 2004, America opened employment for nurses from other countries. I passed my NCLEX and IELTS in 2005 and came to Arizona in January 2006.

America, Here I Come

When I arrived in America, my agency assigned me to Scottsdale HealthCare in Shea, now Honor Health-Shea Medical Center. I came all by myself that time. It was a bit of culture shock as I came from a busy city like Singapore and, with all the convenience of public transportation, arrived in Scottsdale not knowing how to drive and must take the bus that arrives once every hour. This then challenged me to learn how to drive.

The First Time Working in an American Hospital Unit

I was the first Asian to work in our unit. I felt like I was loved by everybody, which is true because I am still working in the same unit for 17 years now. And the teamwork is phenomenal. My contract was for the night shift for two and a half years, and I enjoyed the company of my night colleagues. However, I decided to come to the day shift after my contract ended. I was given a chance to mentor and be a relief supervisor while working on our unit.

When Covid Came

When COVID hit, I was not that concerned for myself because I thought it was the same as taking care of SARS patients.

It was just a deja'vu of my SARS experience in Singapore. But it was never easy seeing my patients suffering from a disease that no one knew the exact treatment yet that time.

Wisdom When Starting as a Nurse in America

In America, a nurse should be more assertive. One may encounter problematic families, and there are difficulties in dealing with them, yet respect and kindness should be afforded to them. Whenever there is an established rapport with the patient and family, they see things differently, and they won't give you much difficulty. And at least be a part of your unit committee. That is one way to develop yourself personally and professionally.

In Career Ladder

As I mentioned, I pursued nursing for economic reasons, but it is my passion for caring and helping others that I stayed in this profession. I always feel that caring for patients is very rewarding. I always say that I wanted to retire as a bedside nurse, but I feel that I am being called for another purpose. A purpose not far from my passion, it's the joy of caregiving, and I named my company, MyTrueJoy. With mission and vision will be achieved through the application of our core values of CARING:

C-comfort
A-affection
R-respect
I-integrity
N-nurture
G-generosity

Parting Words

When adversities and challenges come your way, keep going and believe that when you think it is over, God will send you miracles. And my life's inspiration comes from Mother Teresa's poem, "If you are honest and sincere, people may deceive you. Be honest and sincere anyway. If you find serenity and happiness, some may be jealous. Be happy anyway. The good you do today will often be forgotten tomorrow. Be good anyway. You see, in the end, it is between you and God. It was never between you and them anyway."

****

Nursing is an art: and if it is to be made an art, it requires an exclusive devotion as hard a preparation as any painter's or sculptor's work; for what is having to do with dead canvas or dead marble, compared with having to do with the living body, the temple of God's spirit? It is one of the Fine Arts: I had almost said, the finest of Fine Arts.

-Florence Nightingale

CHAPTER TWO

A FATHER AT 17, NOW A US RN

CHRISTIAN PAULO G.
Bicol

GROWING UP

I had three siblings. I am the middle child in the family. All my siblings are in the medical field. They are all nurses. I am the only one who went abroad. My mom is a plain housewife, and my dad was a Municipal Agricultural Officer. Growing up, we have enough in terms of being able to afford to go to school and eat.

I graduated elementary and high school at La Consolacion and went to college at Camarines Sur. I was a government scholar, so I only paid half of the tuition. The entrance to this school is hard. It is a laddered curriculum; I must be a midwife first before becoming a registered nurse.

After graduation, I supported myself. My other siblings, who were also nurses in the city hospital, were working in Disaster Risk Management in our municipality.

A Teenager Dad

In 2011, my child (firstborn) came to the USA. My dream was to see her. The Story was like this, in 2006, I was 17 years old. I got married to my childhood sweetheart. We were in second year college when we got married and had a baby. Life was hard. I had to ask my parents for milk for the baby and provide my then wife, a US citizen. She decided to come to America with our baby. She applied to the Air force while she was in America. We got divorced when she met her second husband, who was also in the Air Force with her.

Life After College Graduation

After I graduated from college, I left home and worked in a medical center. I gained experience, and after two years, I went to Libya. This was in 2013. Before I left for Libya in 2013, I took first the NCLEX (National Council Licensure Examination) for Registered Nurses in 2011, and I passed. Still, due to retrogression, I was not able to come to America right away. I applied to work in other countries while waiting for my papers to come so that I could provide for myself.

In Libya

This was the place where I met my current wife. In 2013, this was post-war. This was after the president was killed. The struggles were different here. There was only one way to get out of my country and work, so I gambled even though I knew it was unsafe as the effects of war were still there. The environment at that time, as I saw it, was chaotic and unstable. One time the staff was sent home because the militia threatened to take over our hospital. We heard gunshots, but we couldn't do anything. We had to work. I stayed in Libya for four years. I met my wife there, and my child was born in Libya in 2016.

Balikbayan (Going Back To The Philippines)

In 2017, we decided to go back to the Philippines. The ISIS terrorist group took over Libya. I was working in the Intensive Care Unit at that time.

I was back in the Philippines for five months and took my chances to go to Saudi Arabia again because I did not want to have a working gap in my resume. In Saudi, I worked in the Intensive Care Unit.

I was in Saudi Arabia when the pandemic hit. The 38-bed capacity became a 98-bed capacity during our time. My wife came to Saudi Arabia after, but we left my child with my mother-in-law in Isabela. She was two years old at that time, and we never saw her milestones since we were only allowed to go home once a year. In Saudi Arabia, I honed my skills in that place. I became a Senior staff. I Took ECMO (Extracorporeal Membrane Oxygenation) patients, did dialysis, and became a member of the Rapid Response Team Nurse.

In October 2021, I went back to the Philippines. Before I went abroad to another country, I had already applied to come to America. I received an interview at the US Embassy and was issued an immigrant visa. I went back to Saudi Arabia to finish my contract, then flew from there to the US.

Coming to America and the Challenges

In January 2022, I flew to the USA. I stayed for two months in Florida for training and credentialing. My challenge was that I was licensed in California, and it took time for my license to be endorsed. My money was running out. I was not working. The Agency that I was contracted with gave us $270/week. After a few months, they sent me to Arizona. This was in March 2022. The agency allowed me to stay in Tucson with my batch mate. He was already working when I stayed with him. After a month, the agency sent me to Prescott, Arizona.

I did not want to stay with my batch mate for a long time. I felt like I was a burden to him. Finally, in May 2022, I started to work in the hospitals in the valley.

It was hard to adjust at first. I did not have anyone to talk to. I just cried, and my wife was in Saudi. We have different time zones. It was hard, and I was depressed. It was too stressful.

First Time Working In An American Hospital

I worked with a hospital in the Intensive Care Unit abroad. It was challenging there. In the US, I worked in Level 1 trauma, large capacity, and high acuity care. As an international nurse, it was hard. I have nine years of experience as an Intensive Care Unit nurse, but my exposure was different. They treated me not like a new graduate that needed to see how everything worked but as an experienced one. It was a totally different experience from my Intensive Care Unit in another country.

I felt like I experienced professional bullying. The one who was mentoring me was rude. They think that I have nine years of experience and that I should know well. They gave me a preceptorship instead of three months to only two months. I overcame the challenges, but I told the agency that the area was so stressful. The agency was understanding. I told them that I felt that I could not cope. They placed me in another sister facility of the original one. Here, I did two months of preceptorship and got along with the nurses. It was a good community. The staff was supportive and less toxic. It was a 24-bed capacity ICU, and I adjusted very well. I was even awarded the Best Nurse for the month of November. I was new, and they saw my potential.

Right now, I am happy in the workplace with the blessing of God.

My wife will take the NCLEX soon. (After this interview, Paulo's wife took the NCLEX and passed.)

No Guts, No Glory

While coming to America, you need a lot of courage. When you start in America, you start good as zero. You do not have a support system. If you don't have your family here, then you are all alone here.

How To Survive When You Are New In The Workplace

God must have known my struggles when I met Kuya Don at Walmart, and he invited me to come to this church where I met Filipinos. With this, I found a new family. They welcomed me and guided me with my ways and journeys.

With what happened to me in the beginning, I talked to my manager and the coordinator for the whole nurses of the hospital System. I told them my experience, and I told the ADEX (my agency) and the one in charge of the international nurses. I told them that, based on my experience, I experienced professional bullying, and the preceptor was so strict. Since we came from a different setting, we should be treated as new graduates of the system. Based on the experience that I had, they established something so that the new nurses coming here would not experience the same experience that I had.

Words of Wisdom

I realized after graduation that those who become successful are not really those who are so smart during college days, but that success can be achieved from the strategies that you do in life.

CHAPTER THREE

IT IS NEVER TOO OLD TO COME TO AMERICA

ANN B.

Zamboanga City

MY STORY

I grew up in Zamboanga City. We rented a house near the cemetery. We lived very simply. My dad used to buy and sell gold. I have two brothers, and I am the eldest. Growing up, my parents were strict. I understand them being strict so they can give me a better life. I went to a private Catholic School called Immaculate for my elementary and high school years and later to a State University for my college education.

When I was little, I wanted to be a dentist. I did not want to tell my parents I wanted to be a dentist because I knew they could not afford it. So after high school, I saw that my classmates went to take the exam at Western Mindanao State University. They took nursing. I did not study, so when I took the Nursing Aptitude Test (NAT), I failed.

So, I ended up taking psychology. I did not want to retake nursing at that time. When I was in my third year of college, my friends decided to shift to nursing. So, we all decided to take nursing after we passed the NAT (Nursing Aptitude Test). I graduated two years behind my classmates. I graduated with BSN in 1995.

Life After Nursing School

I took my licensure exam, and I passed. I volunteered for three months. When you volunteer, there is no pay. Then, I did not have any job for a long time. There is no nursing job in my place. In 1995, I was able to get a job as a School Nurse at the Department of Education. I was assigned to about 10 – 20 schools. After eight months of working as a school nurse, I got laid off, but the contract was resumed a couple of months after.

By then, in 1996, I got married to my now husband, Robert. I also enrolled as a Special Education teacher; I took one semester, but I did not finish.

What Made You Decide To Come to America? What Were the Challenges you Faced?

I wanted to have a better future. Financially it was hard to prepare to come to work in America. It took a lot of financial effort. I did not worry about preparing myself intellectually, like the test itself. Instead, I had to worry and prepare financially because of the cost of the tests that we needed to take. We don't have any testing centers in Zamboanga City, so I have to go to another city to take the test, and it would cost us more. I have to travel by plane, which will take about 1 hour and planes are more expensive, or go via a large boat which is cheaper but will take about three days to reach my destination.

I have to prepare for the Commission on Graduate of Foreign nursing School (CGFNS), which costs about a month's salary. Then I have to prepare for the NCLEX (National Council Licensure Examination). Then I have to pay for my visa screen. You must have the test for Spoken English (TSE) and IELTS (International English Language Testing System) before a visa screen will be issued. In all, you have to pass three exams before a visa can be processed. What if we fail in one of those, then we have to take and retake again. Sometimes, one test expires before I can take the other test again.

I took my NCLEX from Wisconsin State. As they said, this state has a fast-processing time. It took a couple of years for me to be able to complete the requirements.

First Time In America

When I came to America, my concern was the bedside nursing. I felt I did not have a lot of experience, though I had been a nurse for more than twenty years. I felt I needed to be more confident. The hospital provided preceptorship and orientation, which helped me a lot. I succeeded by praying. Every time I came to work, I prayed a lot. I also didn't know how to drive, so I had to ask my husband or son to drive me.

How Did You Overcome This Challenge?

I prayed a lot. After five years, I now feel that I can do it. I even had a double job in the beginning, but now I only have one job. The hospital called us a lot to do overtime. We were new, so we had the lowest salary, and they always called us for overtime.

During Covid

During COVID, my challenge was how not to get sick from COVID. I still got sick, but it was during the latter part of COVID. I had to protect myself. I used all the necessary precautions.

The saddest thing that happened was that my mom and aunt in the Philippines died several days apart. My aunt was found dead in her home. Several days later, my mom died of COVID. This was in 2021, and I did not get so see them.

Words of Wisdom

Do not give up on your dream to come to America or any dream you have, no matter what the obstacles are. It will happen only in His time. I started the journey of coming to America in 2005. It was ten years later that I was able to come. That was in 2015. I was 44 years old by then. One is never too old to do it.

CHAPTER FOUR

A FLIGHT ATTENDANT, NOW A US RN

J. C. M.
Pampanga

MY STORY

I was born in Pampanga. I live in Angeles City, Pampanga. I'm the youngest. I have three sisters and one brother. My mom and dad were doing business, selling gas. It is a buy and sell of gas for jeepneys. They also had a carinderia (cafeteria) and sari -sari store. I grew up helping my mom and watching the store. I finished elementary school in Teodoro P. Tinio. I used to walk to school together with my friends. For High school, I went to Holy Spirit, a private school.

Why Nursing

My first choice was tourism. However, My mom told me that she already enrolled me in nursing but I wanted to shift to Tourism.

My mom told me, "If I see that you can't handle it, then I'll let you shift ." So, I did not focus on my studies at first, but my mom had an American dream for me.

In my first year as a nursing student, I failed two subjects. I was so happy I failed. That means I can transfer to Tourism. My mom did not get angry; instead, she told me, "Napasa mo yong ibang subjects. Makuha mo rin yon. (You passed the other subjects. You will get it.)" If I had known my mom would not let me shift my course, I would have improved my grades better.

I wanted to go to Manila to enroll in nursing so I won't be late and could graduate with my classmates, but my mom did not allow me.

I had to wait for one year to take the subjects that I failed. I continued my nursing journey as my mom did not let me change my major. Eventually, I developed my love for nursing. I graduated nursing in 2013 and passed my board in 2013 too.

Reality After Graduating from Nursing

After taking the board exam, while waiting for the result to come, I worked in the call center in Angeles City. After one year, once I knew I passed the board exam, I finished my contract.

After I passed my board exam, since I could not find work as a nurse, I worked as a volunteer at Raphael Foundation Medical City in Angeles. I worked as a volunteer nurse for six months. While working as a Volunteer, I received 2,000 to 4,000 pesos a month ($36 -$72) dollars a month.

After six months, I saw that my friend applied and was waiting to work as a flight attendant. I saw that Emirates was hiring a Cabin Service Attendant. I went to Manila and lined up at 4:00 am. I did not pass as an assistant to the flight attendants. I did not give up. I saw that Oman Air was also hiring, so I applied as a flight attendant. I waited for the visa for three months. They were not updating their system. When they updated, they changed their requirements to 22 years old. I was only 21. I was heartbroken. I was excited, but I did not make it because of my age.

I did not give up. I applied again. This time to Saudia Airlines. My sister would drive from Pampanga to Manila, which could take hours. I finally passed, and in November 2014, I was finally a flight attendant.

Life As A Flight Attendant

I felt like life was ok. Now I have money. I feel there is a new purpose in life for me from God. As flight attendants, we have training for two months, but this is a paid salary. After four months, I went home to the Philippines. I would fly to the Philippines. I would have five consecutive days off to spend time with my family. Though I was a flight attendant, I felt happier as a nurse. I ended up working as a flight attendant for five years and six months. At one point, I wanted to resign and become a medical doctor. I gave up the dream of becoming a doctor because no one could support me. I needed to work and support my family.

Hardest Time Of My Life

May 2015 was the hardest time of my life. It was my first visit back to the Philippines after the training I had as a flight attendant. My mom was excited to see me. She said my sister wanted to be a flight attendant, but she did not become one. I consider my sister as my idol, so I pursued the dream. One of my mom's dreams was to see me wearing my flight attendant uniform, so when I landed in the Philippines, I did not change my uniform. I saw my mom in my uniform, and it was a joyful reunion.

The day I went home was a get-together with my family, but it was mixed with sadness later. We wanted to go to Star City, Pampanga then later; my mom said she wanted to go to San Simeon. This City is 1 to 1.5 hours away. We couldn't do both. She decided to go to Star City.

That night when we returned home, she was having some health issues. We brought her to the hospital, and she was diagnosed with

Diabetic Ketoacidosis (DKA). After Three days, she felt she was ok, but later she got a cardiac arrest. I was still visiting my mom in the hospital when she got the cardiac arrest.

They later transferred her to ICU (Intensive Care Unit). I used to work in this hospital, so they let me go into the ICU to watch her. In ICU, the medicine costs a lot. It was about 4,000 pesos ($72.00) to 6,000 pesos ($109.00) a day.

As I watched her in ICU, there was a change, and I could not wake her up. It took a while for the nurses to come, so I had to give my mom my first real-life CPR (Cardio Pulmonary Resuscitation). They did everything they could while she was in the hospital. She did not survive. Me and my sister ended up with huge bills. We did not have a lot of money to pay the bills. I was sad, she only waited to see me back, and she died. It was my first time going home after being trained to be a flight attendant when she died.

Finding The Love of My Life

When I separated from my ex-boyfriend, I met my ex-college boyfriend, Mr. P, again. One day he messaged me. He told me he would look at my Facebook page once in a while. He said, Kapag bumalik pa ako sa buhay niya, I won't let her go. (If I come back into his life, he will not let me go.)

Mr. P is also a nurse, but he is not working as a nurse but has worked in one of the luxury ships abroad. We have a long distance relationship, but he was already telling me he wanted to settle, so we got married within a couple of months. In Mr. P, I saw myself getting married. Finally, we got married in 2019 and had a daughter later.

I went back to work as a flight attendant, but COVID came, and I was asked to take COVID leave. When I was in the Philippines, I wanted to make sure I still had my nursing skills, so I worked as a nurse in one of the hospitals. I stayed in the Philippines for three months, and by then, Saudia called me again to work in the airline.

Coming To America

I really wanted to come to the USA, but when I knew that I could not be a doctor, I changed my perspective and worked on being a nurse.

I was in a long-term relationship, and my focus, in the beginning, was not on the NCLEX, but on the things that we wanted, so I failed the NCLEX. I was not certain or sure what my priorities were. I took the NCLEX the second time, and finally, in August 2021, I passed the NCLEX. I paid everything for my review. I am waiting now for the hospital to tell me when I can work. I came with a visa and found a hospital sponsor who was willing to petition me.

(She has started working since this interview in one of the hospitals that sponsored her.)

Challenges In America

The hardest part of my situation is that I cannot go back to the Philippines whenever I want since I have to change my visa status. I left my child, who was one year old, and I could not hold or touch her. I do call her every day. Was it worth coming to America? Yes, it is for the future of my family. It is worth it.

Words of Wisdom

Never give up on the dream that you have. It might take some detours, but it will all surely come together in the end.

CHAPTER FIVE

A NURSE LEADER

EMMA R.

Luzon

I came to America in 1989. My first stop was in Chicago, where I went for a few days to meet my parents and sister. On Feb 14, I came to Phoenix, AZ.

My Childhood

I think I have a happy childhood. My mother is a hardworking wife, and my father was a teacher, and later when he came to America, he worked as a security guard while my mother in the Philippines owned a little store in the market. I helped her sell fruit juice in the market.

I grew up and was born in Tanay, Rizal. Later I came to America. I visited sometime my mother's hometown in Vigan. I came to America on a fiancée visa. Though I have a petition from my father since he had a stroke, I have to come here early. I accepted his proposal. So, I came here right then instead of two years later.

Struggles In Coming To America

I did not have any agency because it was a fiancée visa. Life is always a challenge, but I think the challenges from God only strengthen me. Always pray. Always turn to God whatever problems you have. One of my challenges when I was in America, I would say discrimination, but I did not have that many friends. During my first three years at work, I was bullied.

I left those challenges behind me, and I don't have any regret. Whatever the challenges were, I went through them courageously, with no regret or resentment. I wanted to live a happy life.

Challenges In Coming to America

I was a very blessed person. When I was interviewed, I brought all the letters from my husband and pictures. My application said I was a registered nurse. So, they asked a personal question about my husband and how we met. When they knew I was an RN, it was a regular conversation about the nursing staff. He asked me what to do about a certain condition, so I thought it was not a challenge.

My First Day At Work in An American Hospital

Since I just came here to Arizona. I did not work for weeks or probably a month. I felt so bored while waiting for my NCLEX OR CGFNS first. I applied through an agency and worked as a CNA (Certified Nursing Assistant). I worked in a St Joseph facility in a nursing home. My first day was 8-hour work, and during lunch time, my husband happened to call me and ask how I was doing. My coworker did not tell me that my husband called.

After 8 hours of work, they informed me about my husband's call. I went to the nurse's station, and they told me that I could not use the phone. They told me to go downstairs and use 25 cents to call him back. I felt discriminated against. I worked so hard for 8 hours. I did not go back.

During Covid

I was already retired. I volunteered at the State Farm and gave COVID vaccination. I also volunteered in pharmaceutical places,

ASIAN pacific organizations, and elderly homes to provide boosters and Covid vaccines. During COVID, we have to reach out to our members to give appreciation to our members. We gave them Christmas gifts during COVID.

Words of Wisdom

Throughout my life, I really believed in God, the Almighty, and that whatever we ask him for, we receive it sooner or later and that his doors are always open for us. Whatever successes my children have, it's because GOD gave it to me. All the material things that GOD gave me was an instrument to help others.

There is a saying that giving is better than receiving because you don't anticipate getting it back, but it does. GOD loves us. Let GOD be the center of our lives.

Enjoy life, do not dwell on some sentiments. Whatever you can, help others do it. Sometimes there would be regrets if you won't be able to help. That would be a good one for me. The world is full of challenges, but we can have a happy life together.

Note: Emma served in various leadership positions in the community. As a nurse leader, she served as the President of the Philippines Nurses Association of Arizona.

CHAPTER SIX

DESTINED TO BE A NURSE

Julie Ann

Luzon

Born and raised in the Philippines. I am the youngest of seven children. I have five sisters and one brother. My mother is a Grade School teacher (Mena Pascual). My Dad is Inocencio Bautista. He worked at The Chest Center in Cabanatuan City as an X-ray technician.

I initially wanted to be a doctor, but my oldest sister convinced me that Nursing is a very rewarding career, and I absolutely agree! I studied Bachelor of Science in Nursing at the Chinese General Hospital College of Nursing.

Family of Nurses

My sisters are my inspiration. One would say caring is in our blood. All of us six sisters are nurses. My aunts and uncles are mostly medical providers.

I worked at the University of Santo Thomas Hospital in Manila right after Graduation. Got here in the United States in 1994, H1 Visa. It wasn't easy starting life here in America. Missed my life in the Philippines, plus I had to work as a Nursing Assistant in a Nursing Home setting while waiting to take NCLEX. It was a culture shock for me. We do not have a nursing home in the Philippines. We take care of our parents and grandparents and older relatives at home.

I was one of the first batch of Nurses that took the Computerized NCLEX. I answered seventy-five questions, and then the computer stopped. I was so nervous, but I know God has plans for me, for all of us.

I'm fortunate to have my oldest sister and her family. They took us in and helped me and my other friends when we got here in America. We lived with them until we were able to stand on our own feet.

Meeting my Husband, Starting a Family

I met my husband at my sister's home. He was there with his mom, attending a Filipino Association meeting. He was born in the Philippines. His mom went to America right after she gave birth to my husband and his twin brother. They were four years old when they were able to reunite with their parents.

We had our trials and challenges when we started having our family. I had two miscarriages before I was able to have our first born. We didn't lose faith in God; I believe that He wouldn't give us any trials we cannot handle. He blessed us with four healthy children.

Career

Here in America, I started working in a nursing home. I later worked in one of the hospitals and Home Health in the Northwest Suburbs of Chicago. When we moved to Arizona, I worked at Hospital and then eventually at a Government Medical Center. I want to serve those who served this Country.

Plan In life

I will hopefully, slow down or retire in the next 3-5 years when all four children graduate from college. So far, our oldest son and one of the twin daughters already graduated.

During Covid

Covid played a huge impact on everybody's life. I was lucky enough to be working from home in 2019. It was Tele work. Our goal was to take care of veterans and make sure they were seen and getting appropriate care, making sure they got the best care. Covid still affected me, and the vaccine caused some irregularity in my heart. I got really sick when I contracted Covid December 2020 and ended up in the Emergency Room with chest pain and shortness of breath, having Bigeminy, Diagnosed with Covid Pneumonia. My cardiac condition didn't improve. I am still dealing with abnormal heart rhythms.

What Were the Challenges You Encountered in America?

I overcame many challenges in life. At one point in our life, we had four kids, four y/o and under, all in diapers and drinking milk. It wasn't easy to balance life and work. It was hard with four kids. Without my cousin's help, we couldn't make it. She's like a second mother to our children. My husband worked during the day, and I worked the night shift for 14 years.

The wisdom you like to Impart to our nurses who are in America and Those Who are About to Come

You have to have a big heart; you cannot do nursing for money. You have to have a satisfying job. I worked for hospice. I did community service in Illinois, and it was a gratifying job. I was doing the end of life. I was on call from 7 am in the morning. I will call the examiner if I need to. Then we would do suction and catheter. Whenever they will call me, the family would need support for end of life, or if the patient is dying, I will go, driving and walking in the snow. I did this until I came to Arizona. I did this for almost four years.

You need to have faith, perseverance and patience to make it.

You also have to have a big heart, understand that there's a reason for everything.

CHAPTER SEVEN
NURSING AS MY SECOND CAREER. A NURSE INFORMATICS

EMILY B.(Manila)

I was born in Manila in Oct 1970. I was told that during that time, typhoon Yoling (remember back then, all the typhoons were named females) was in full force, so the hospital was on the generator, and to help out, oil lamps were used. I heard the babies had soot on their noses in the morning...lol).

I grew up in Cubao, Quezon City, but I remember always going to my lolo and Lola's (maternal side) "house" in Sampaloc, Manila, every weekend. I say "house" in quotes because my Lolo was the all-around at the public elementary school (i.e., he was security, custodian, camera man for student ids, etc., so he was allowed to live at the school with his family). Imagine, the whole school was our playground. We played with our cousins.

There were four girls in the family, and I was #2. An interesting note is that I, #2, was born left-handed (now ambidextrous though, since back then, the nuns at school would swat the hands of left-handed kids when they caught them writing with the Left hand forcing them to switch to the right. Of course, they don't really monitor recess, so I played jacks with my left hand, the same as#4, our youngest. I am 10 years older than the youngest, so by the time she went to school, they never did force her to switch. My mom is also left-handed (she was #3 in her family of 8 siblings). So, like us, it was also alternate per child (i.e., L-R-L (my mom), R- then the bottom four kids R-L-R-L).

My dad was a TV commercial director. Prior to directing, he was a radio announcer, radio producer, etc.) Sadly, he passed away at age 44.

School Days

I remember going to a small neighborhood school for preschool, then on to Dominican College in San Juan, Manila, for formal elementary and High School. For College, I went to the University of Santo Tomas (UST is another Dominican-run institution. So I was truly Dominican-bred), where I got my Bachelor of Arts Major in Communication Arts in 1991.

Going to School in America

In the US, when I decided to take up nursing so many years later, I did my pre-requisite courses at Phoenix College (which was closest to where I lived previously). There was a 2 to 3semester wait for Nursing School at Maricopa County, so after I finished my prerequisites and submitted my application for nursing school, I had to wait 2 to 3 semesters to get in. I had to put down several Maricopa County Community College District (MCCCD) schools that offer nursing versus just one so I had better chances of starting nursing school.

I got accepted into the school that was the last of my choices Estrella Mountain Community College (EMCC). My class was the 1st graduating class for RNs. Previously they only offered LPN classes) since it was pretty far from where I lived, although closer to the house that we were building by the time I got accepted. It was a 4-semester course, and in the summer after the 1st two semesters, I also took some classes (instead of vacationing/resting) that will give me enough credits to be an LPN (although I was not planning to take the exams it was just a back-up plan in case I didn't finish/pass nursing).

It was tough going back to school full-time after having graduated college back in 1991. Taking pre-requisites while working full time as a Systems Analyst wasn't a big deal as I was only taking a few classes here and there. Starting the Nursing program requires my full attention, so I had to quit my IT (Information Technology) job. Luckily, I didn't have to use my back-up plan. I graduated in 2010 with an Associate in Applied Science - Nursing. In 2015, I graduated with my Master in Science - Nursing with a specialization in Informatics.

What Motivated You To Take up Nursing?

Nursing was not my first choice. Back when I was in the Philippines when I was in high school, I entertained the thought of going into Law School (UP) or Dentistry. However, I opted for a degree in Communication Arts to go into Advertising. This was a "safe and practical" choice on my part.

As I mentioned previously, my dad died at age 44. I was a sophomore in HS, while our eldest was a senior in HS. She was going to be a doctor. With her four years of pre-med, and if I pursue Dentistry, she will go to Med School proper while I will go into Dental School proper at the same time. My mom would not be able to afford it. Actually, I should say that it would be too much for my grandpa to shoulder. We were in the Philippines he helped us big time by sending us money (this was after the insurance money my dad left us was gone. My mom tried to make it last by investing, but that turned out to be a bad decision, and used up the money. It was my grandpa to the rescue. My Lolo (grandpa) came to the US when he was almost 60 years old. He worked two jobs and sent us money to help us.

After working in IT for eight years (15 years total in the hotel industry), I wanted to work in a field where what I do matters more on a personal level, whether directly or indirectly. And with the practical side of me, I also wanted a job that would be close (if not more) to what I was making in IT, but instead of the usual salary, I wanted an hourly job where I could get paid overtime. I am a workaholic and always end up working a lot of hours, which is unfortunate when you are in a salaried position.

What Was Your Work After Nursing School? How Was it Like to Work in the USA?

I graduated nursing at a very bad time. Previously there were talks of a nursing shortage here in the US, but that was not the case when I graduated. The economy was in a bad place, and we were still reeling from the effects of the real estate crash in 2008. Nurses who were supposed to retire are not retiring (needing to recoup their 401 Ks). It took me a while to get a job. Most of the places had "not accepting new grads in their posting." There were Home Health agencies available, but as a new grad, I wasn't comfortable going into Home Health and being by myself. I was finally able to land a job doing vaccination clinics for Mollen Immunizations. It was a seasonal job, so in parallel, I was also looking. I finally got into an SNF/LTC (Skilled Nursing Facility /Long Term Care Facility) place as a pool nurse. They were very nice and gave me a lot of shifts.

When Did You Decide To Come to America? Tell Us About Your Journey.

My story is personal, and I'll tell you in detail when we see each other ☺. Let me say that I am almost on my 30th year of vacation here in the US.

What Sacrifices Did You Do To Come to the USA?

No sacrifices at all. Relatives on both sides, father's and mother's side, are in the US. My paternal side is mainly in Chicago/Illinois area, while my maternal side is in AZ, so I was not lonely.

What Was Your Destination ? Phoenix, AZ

Your First Job in USA. What Were the Challenges?

My 1st job in the US is non-nursing. It was a call center. Nursing-wise - my first job was in the immunization area. Sometimes, my accent would get in the way as I was not easily understood.

Tell us About your Career Ladder.

My first stint as a nurse was for Mollen Immunizations doing vaccination clinics in various areas, mostly retail spaces. Initially, for every clinic, there would be a nurse and an assistant. The assistant handles the cash, insurance verifications, etc. Towards the end, they cut back on the assistants, and so the nurse would have to do everything (set up, verify forms, get insurance, handle cash, keep track of inventory, breakdown, report, etc.) After that, I did SNF/LTC, Chronic Disease Management via Telephonic Nursing, then Informatics Analyst, and most recently as Clinical Informatics Manager

A Nurse During COVID

When COVID hit, I was working at Valleywise Health (previously known as Maricopa Integrated Health System [MIHS], aka Maricopa County Hospital). I was a Clinical Informatics Analyst nurse. We were one of the first ones to work from home. There were a lot of unknowns then.

I remember our CMIO sharing the Johns Hopkins website that showed the world map and toe Covid counts, and we were glued to it. One of the things I was directly working on with another analyst related to Covid was setting up virtual visits for families, primarily for our Behavioral Health (BH) patients, and other units as well, but we started with BH.

Thank goodness we had iPhones available that we have used for 15-minute safety checks (via EPIC's ROVER application), and so we had hardware readily available for BH. We did have to order tablets for other units, though). It was quite challenging dealing with educating staff, family as well as dealing with wireless signals.

Words of Wisdom

Nursing is a great profession to be in. It is a field that allows you to wear many different hats without having to leave the profession. If you get worn out from doing bed-side nursing, there's teaching, research, clinical adjunct, informatics, etc. While nursing pays good, it is hard work. Expect and be prepared to work hard.

******

"Let us never consider ourselves finished nurses…We must be learning all of our lives." *–Florence Nightingale.*

CHAPTER EIGHT

A TV COMMUNICATION STAFF, A NURSE MANAGER NOW

SONIA S

SAMAR

Childhood Memories

I grew up in Calbayog, Samar, Philippines. My mom was a teacher and a dressmaker. My dad was a tailor. I have a simple childhood. I am used to studying all the time. Looking back, I realized my dad probably had OCD (Obsessive Compulsive Disorder). Everything had to be super clean and tidy (laughing).

I have two brothers and a sister. I am the youngest. My oldest sister is 12 years older than me. I went to a public school for elementary, and in high school, I went to a catholic school.

In elementary school, I was branded as a tomboy. There were bullies in the school who would hide our slippers, and I would go after them. I punched the scariest kid in school in the face and was called to the principal's office, but my teacher/adviser defended me because the kid was known to be a bully.

After high school, I went to the University of Santo Tomas. I had to take exams to apply as a working scholar. I was convinced by my sister to study Mass Communications even if I really wanted to study Foreign Affairs. As a working scholar, I worked in the library in the morning and then at night at the school I went to school.

Life After College

As my first job after college, I worked at the National Commission Concerning Disabled Persons (NCCDP). I was the Public Information assistant. At that time, the company was new, and in the Philippines, there was no public knowledge about disability and how to treat disabled persons. I wrote articles and created slide presentations about disability and awareness of how to treat them and give them respect. I was involved in community outreach campaigns. It was a really good and fulfilling job.

I left NCCDP to teach at St Louis University in Baguio City, but because I had to wait for the second semester, I ended up working in the former TV station, Channel 4. I was a production assistant for the TV shows "Patok Na Patok" and "Love Lea," which starred Lea Salonga, who at that time was very young. I also was a game coordinator and created games for TV, so I would ask my friends to join as guests on the shows.

Meeting the Love of My life.

In 1981, as destined by our fate, my former elementary classmate and I met by accident in our hometown. We both graduated from college in Manila but never saw each other after elementary. Seeing each other from 6th grade to after college was a complete surprise. Never knew that was the day I was to start seeing my future husband. I was 23 years old then when I saw him again in Samar. I thought that was the end of the casual encounter when we returned to Manila, but I didn't realize it was the beginning of a friendship that was meant to be a lifelong relationship. If you ask him, he has a different version (laughing.) He would jokingly tell friends that the moment I saw him that day,

I never stopped trying to get his attention by going to church every day so I could pass by their house. He has this talent for making up stories but mostly as a joke to tease me.

So, in 1985 we ended up living together. He cannot get married because he was under a petition to come to America. He was petitioned by his mother as single. Therefore, by US law, he must be able to provide a certificate of single status from the national census once the petitioner is called to show up at the US Embassy in Manila.

Living together without the blessings of marriage was devastating to my very Catholic mother and a cousin of the late Cardinal Julio Rosales. He was part of the Rosales family in Calbayog. We could not get married, so she asked the brother, who was Archbishop, to bless us.

We had no choice but to wait for my husband to get petitioned to come to the US, get his green card, and return to the Philippines to marry me and start the petition for me and the children. My mom had passed away before we had the church wedding, but I knew it was important to her to see her daughter get married in the church, so my thoughts were with her during our simple wedding rites.

In 1994, Jerry, my husband, came to the United States. We had one child at that time. He had a green card, and he would come home to the Philippines every year, and each time, he would beg not to return to the US any longer. He would say, "kahit madildil tayo ng asin (sprinkle salt in the food) as long as we are together." We would tell him we want to sprinkle bacon in the food.

In 2001, we came to America. I remember that after our first few weeks, I developed body aches. I called my doctor friend in the Philippines, and she told me, "you never worked while in the

Philippines, and now you have to do everything there. That is where the body ache is coming from."

My husband was able to buy a house for us. My sister-law provided for everything in the house. She bought spoons, forks, and other stuff. I was working in a retail store part-time. After a couple of months, I found out that I was pregnant. I was 42 years old. My husband was speechless for three days. So, my sister-in-law told him that if he didn't stop the drama, they would adopt the baby. He finally got over it.

Journey To Nursing

It was about nine months after the baby that I thought about going back to school. I quit my job in the retail store, and my sister- in-law, who has a care home, helped me go back to school.

I was 44 years old when I started nursing school and graduated at 47 years old in 2006. It was completely different. I had to take the prerequisites, and there was waiting for one semester after I finished the prerequisites.

I came from a traditional way of doing school. I found it hard initially to study for my nursing classes until I and my classmates developed a study group. We helped each other and finally made it through even until we all passed our NCLEX.

What It Was like To Be Working As A Nurse

It was hard, but I was able to adjust easily. I never knew how it was to be a nurse in the Philippines, so all my training was here. I realized then that it must be hard for nurses who came from the Philippines and work here.

I remember precepting a new nurse from the Philippines. She had more experience than me in the Philippines, but she told me that there were no PICC (Peripherally Inserted Central Catheter) lines where she came from. She had no experience in how to insert a G tube (Gastrostomy) feeding. The residents are the ones who were doing it. So, everything was completely new to her.

Nursing Career Pathway

I initially worked as an inpatient nurse, then later, an opportunity to work in the outpatient setting as a PACT nurse was offered, and I thought I should try it. After a year, I applied to get my RN-MSN. In two years, I was done with school. I was told to apply as an assistant nurse manager, then later became the Acting Nurse Manager during COVID. I later applied to become the nurse manager and got the position.

A Nurse During Covid

During COVID, I did a lot in the clinic. I was able to introduce telework. We had a skeleton staffing, and then I presented the telework option. We did not have enough time to plan. We had to detail a lot of nurses to the inpatient unit to support the hospital. Some nurses have not worked as bedside nurses for the last couple of years. I had to do telework to make sure that everything was still functional in the clinic. There were challenges as we didn't have the same staff as we used to because we had to send out staff to the inpatient.

Wisdom To Impart To Those Aspiring To Become A Nurse In America

For me, nursing is about relationships. I never thought I would become a nurse. You have to love what you are doing. It had to come from the heart .

I won the Daisy award (recognition given to the superhuman-work nurses do). I never thought I would get it. I got the award when a patient sent a letter to the hospital and said that no matter how tough my day was, I tried to explain to her all that needed to be done, and she understood what was going on. She noted that my smiles and positive attitude helped ease the anxiety of being in the hospital. It made me appreciate more the work that I was doing. It was rewarding.

Never stop dreaming and aiming for a better life. Nursing is a very noble job where you make a difference in people's lives.

CHAPTER NINE

NO PLACE TO STAY IN NEW YORK. NOW A NURSE PRACTITIONER.

Rachel T.

Luzon

Tell us about your childhood, home life, and struggles growing up. Where did you go to school?

I am the seventh child of nine children. My mother is a teacher, not to mention she was my principal. My father managed a business and our farm. Due to many siblings, we were raised with very strict parents. We lived on a farm and were very religious. We did chores before and after school. Luxury life was not an option. In addition to many siblings, my mother likes to adopt other kids so that they may be sent to school. Though we had nothing, we had to share with other children.

I attended Catholic school for my high school and St Jude's College of Nursing. There was no other choice but to pass. We could not afford to fail. This was the only way to get out of poverty.

What Made You Want To Enroll or Take Nursing?

I never wanted to be a nurse; it was my mother's dream. I was doing my pre-med when I found out that the people I expected to help reach my dream of being a doctor could no longer support me. I had no choice but to follow my mother's dream of nursing. On the other hand, I was told that nursing was the only way to get out of the country. I always wanted to get away, maybe because so many people were at home.

41

What Were Your Struggles in Nursing School?

At first, it was hard to do things you weren't passionate about. In the 1980s, height was a requirement in nursing. They required

5'2" and above, and I am only 5'. I always have to prove myself so that I can be an exception to that rule. I also had to have stellar grades to maintain my scholarship, as nursing was one of the most expensive courses at the time.

Life After Graduating College

I was sent on a mission as part of my commitment to my scholarship. I worked with Mt. Pinatubo victims in Tarlac province to serve the Filipino natives, namely the Negritos. I was there for nine months until I was transferred to the hospital in Manila. Then, I worked for four years in the United Arab Emirates.

What Were the Steps Took and Struggles In Coming to America?

Just like everyone, I had to pass the CGFNS exam and English exam to be able to apply for nursing in America. I applied in 1995, but my application was held after spending money because President Clinton stopped hiring nurses at that time. Reapplication opened up in 2000. I was finally able to go to New York.

Your First Time in America

I was told I didn't have to bring money to America because my job was guaranteed. Upon arrival, I had no place to stay. I had to call a friend to let me stay at their place. At the time, I only had a hundred dollars in my pocket. While I was living with my friend, her husband didn't like my presence in their house as they had to rent the room. I had to leave and look for another place. I found a distant relative to stay with, but I had to babysit their kids at night while I worked on days.

It wasn't easy doing so. I had to ask my employer for a space to live. I stayed in the oxygen storage room for five weeks until I found a roommate to rent an apartment. Unfortunately, my roommate was molested and had to move back to her family. I had to leave New York and move to Virginia, where it was more affordable to stay.

Your First Time In Working In An American Hospital, What Were Your Struggles?

Part of my job offer was to work as an RN right away, and I worked with a permit. On my first day of work, I was told I was a charge nurse in an eighteen-vented unit. I had no experience with ventilators whatsoever. It was a struggle, given that I had no experience with that kind of acuity and the culture of New York staff. I was able to manage with guidance.

Your experience during the time of Covid as a nurse

As a nursing supervisor in a hospital, staffing was a challenge. There were not enough nurses to take care of Covid patients or enough rooms or enough PPE (Personal Protective Equipment) for everyone. That was just the front of fear of getting sick myself. I became an observer of everyone's fear and anger.

In my other job as a CVICU (Coronary Vascular Intensive Care Unit) nurse taking care of ECMO (Extracorporeal Membrane Oxygenation) patients, which is taking care of the sickest patients in the Valley. Prior to COVID time, one ECMO patient is taken care of by two nurses. During COVID, it became one nurse to three patients. There were several deaths in a day due to COVID.

Watching patients die, families grieving, and exhausted front liners felt like a never-ending curse. I also see the beauty of camaraderie in my coworkers.

Your Career Ladder

I have been a nurse for 30 years, 29 of which have been bedside. I am a CCRN (Critical Care Registered Nurse) and CVRN (Cardiovascular Registered Nurse). In 2016, I earned my MSN. In 2021, I earned my FNP. My many positions are scattered through my degrees, including ICU assistant manager, patient safety manager, nursing supervisor, home health nurse, community health nurse, dialysis nurse, registry nurse, heart transplant nurse, and critical care nurse. I currently work as a nurse practitioner for heart failure/heart transplant in the private sector and a primary care nurse practitioner in a transition to practice program in the federal government.

****

"When you're a nurse, you know that every day you will touch a life or a life will touch yours."-Unknown.

CHAPTER TEN

FROM OPERATING ROOM NURSE TO NURSE INFORMATICS

MAINE T.
Zamboanga City

About Me

There were six children in my family, including my mom and dad; there were 8 of us. I am the eldest among my brother and sisters. My family lived in a compound. Half a block from my place was my father's family. So, in terms of family, we were close-knit. In terms of need, there is always help. My grandma watched my brother. Growing up was really fun. Thinking back, I did not think it was easy because you always wanted to play.

There was a lot of struggle, and there were 6 of us siblings. My dad's job was not really stable. My mom was the breadwinner, but in everything, God provided. During high school, the best gift that my dad gave me was to bring me to the fellowship (church), and so that was where I got to know the lord.

School Days

I went to a Chinese school, Zamboanga Chong Hua High School. The kids here were rich kids. My grandma told me not to get too close to the kids so that I won't get jealous. My classmates were good, and we also had the means at that time. During High school, we were beginning to have hardship. This was when I transferred to Western Mindanao State University (WMSU).

I got honors in high school, where I was part of the top ten in the classroom. Around our time were 80 students per class and we had to bring the snacks from the canteen to the classroom. It comes in a bilao (Flat-round shaped rice winnower). There is someone assigned to get the snacks from the canteen. Our canteen was so small, so it will fall if all students will come at once. It was hard at times. We get short in money from the sales.

I was already an entrepreneur; I was selling some stuff. This was also a scary time as there were rebels who invaded the Recom, the military facility. Our school was kind of near the military area. When the rebels invaded this, we were in the school when it happened.

What made you take Nursing?

Mommy was a nurse. But when she graduated, my dad's father was a typical Chinese. My grandpa asked her, why should you go work and leave the country? So, mom worked a little and stopped. Then when she started working when we were in college, she worked as a clinic nurse, the registrar's office then licensing. This was the work where she retired.

Choosing Nursing

It was always on my mind. In terms of financial, nursing was always in demand abroad. Mom was a nurse, and the possibility of going abroad was always at the back of her mind. A lot of batch mates in high school were also taking Nursing, and all my barkadas (friends) were also taking nursing. It was really fun. We went to Manila for a Related Learning Experience (RLE).

What I really loved about college was the clinical, especially going to the community. I learned a lot. I graduated Cum Laude and was a Clinical Proficiency Awardee.

47

In Taking NCLEX and CGFNS

Right now, the CGFNS will not matter now. I had to take CGFNS (Commission on Graduate of Foreign Nursing School), TOEFL (Test of English as Spoken English), and TSE (Test for Spoke English), this was in 1995. I was worried about TSE. They said if your equipment were defective, they would just fail you. So, the combination of this, you have to apply for a certificate, but for the NCLEX, I have to take it in America. In taking the tests, I'm sure my mom and dad helped me pay for the test, but I was also working.

Coming to America

There was always in my mind to come to America. But I think you have to have experience, so I went to Manila. My uncle supported me by letting me stay in his house, and by God's grace, I had a job in the delivery room and operating room that were combined. All the while, I was thinking of coming here.

In 1995, I resigned because I was already scheduled to come to America. This was the time they H1B visa closed. So, I stayed in Zamboanga for a couple of months, then went back to Manila. H1B Visa closed for a while, so I found a health care insurance job ad and applied. I really learned a lot about insurance. So, I stayed in this job until the USA opened gain in 2001, and this was when I Left the Philippines.

In 1999 I remember this because of Y2K. My mom heard about someone who was recruiting nurses. So, I submitted all my requirements. So, when I checked the status of coming to America online, I had to use the Y2K computers. Finally December in 2002, I was finally able to come to the US.

Avenue in Coming to America

It was a recruitment agency here in America that allowed me to come to the USA, but the person I had to pay was the lawyer, and he was the one who made the paper and had a hook up with the agency. It was expensive, and there were no freebies.

The good thing was, we were able to make arrangements and give a little money and the rest we will pay when I start working. During my interview at the embassy, they just asked me about the work.

God was really good. So, the house where I am working in America was very near my aunt's place. My aunt allowed me to stay in their place and housed me.

First Time In America

I came here in December, so I told my aunt in the Philippines that if it is hot, you need to open the air-conditioning; here in America, if it is hot, we just open the windows. Another thing that stood out to me at that time was the steak; you have to tell them what you want, how you want it, and so many choices. In buying coffee, you have so many things to consider.

First Time Working in an American Hospital

Since my aunt housed me, I was not in a hurry to work. We don't have NCLEX yet, so we have to work as Certified Nursing Assistants. One of the things that stood out when I started working was my work as a Certified Nursing Assistant. My patient was huge, and I had to turn her in, and it was really hard. I realized then how hard the work was, so I told the agency If I could stay home and just study for NCLEX.

It was around this time that I hooked up with my classmate Sheila and I learned that I could work without waiting for NCLEX, so I worked in the nursing home until I got my license. So around six months, I have to wait. So, after I passed, the agency gave me some training and brought me to some colleges to have the training.

So, it was funny how you get assigned to an area. You draw lots. So, I was assigned to Mission Hospital on the Oncology unit. My first hospital experience was really great. I had great mentors and charge nurses. I even have some connections even now. During the contract, I stayed for two years under the agency. After the contract, the hospital hired me. It was a smooth transition from my work from 2001 to 2010. I moved to different areas from Oncology. I went to OR. It was easy because, in the Philippines, the Delivery Room had some OR.

Challenges Working in An American Hospital

It was really lonely. In a way, I had a family. I remember it was lonely because I called my parents every day. I had the budget, and there was no Facebook. So, to conquer the loneliness, I worked a lot. If there were people who needed holidays, I worked a lot, so I just worked to conquer this loneliness. So, my cousin, when I moved to this apartment, she moved with me, but we didn't see each other as she was working the day shift, and I was night, so I just placed some post-it notes to communicate.

So the apartment we got was sponsored by the agency, but there was no TV, so we had to use a 5-inch TV, a tiny one. So, the salary in 2001 was not a lot. I still have to pay for my lawyer.

I was blessed because my uncle taught me to drive before I left the house and my cousin. When I got the car, I already knew how to drive. I became the designated driver for the batch of nursing recruits. There were about five of us. We schedule weekends to get the grocery.

So, we place it in the trunk, and we separate who would get it.

Career Ladder

So, I started in Medical Oncology. There was an opportunity for reentry for OR. So, in the OR during that time, they transitioned into a new system. While in the Philippines, I was really interested in computers. There was a time I, Nelma, and Lida joined an excel training. So, the computer was on my radar.

Because of my experience in the OR, that was how I got the position at the CLINICOMP (a software company), and their clients were the DOD and VA hospitals. During my time in the OR, there were people coming in, so I dealt with them. They travel all the time, and I started applying. Eventually, I found this company thru indeed that was stationed in San Diego. They gave me the chance to start my informatics career for ten years.

As an informatics nurse, it was cool to see the coming together of a system from the view of the nurse to bring it to be developed on the technical side. Because you understand nursing, now you can explain to the technical team what is needed.

You go to the hospital and interview their needs then you develop. After you train the nurses and then you go Live. You then handle the accounts of the different hospitals assigned to you.

I started as a clinical analyst, then became a senior clinical analyst, then team lead, and later became a director.

COVID TIME

During the pandemic, travel stopped, so I went back to work in the hospital. While in Informatics, I traveled almost every week. There was also international travel, like in Japan I stayed for three weeks straight. I traveled to about 35 States in the USA as an informatics. I was able to go to the USA side of Cuba as part of my job. These all stopped during the pandemic.

In 2020 this was the time of the pandemic, and the company let me go. I had my surgery then and was gone for a while. There was nothing to work on. The company gave me a good package, and I found work again in the Medical Oncology unit where I worked when I first came to the US. I started work in January, and by April, my eyes went bad. I needed to stop working.

To add to my journey, people asked me about my husband. In 2003, I met my husband, and he was really supportive. Even though there were people around me, I still felt lonely, so the Lord gave me my husband so I could have somebody.

Right now, I am just so blessed by all the experiences of having to travel and see places. I also see friends when I travel. I am so thankful that GOD enriched my life during these two years of how He provided for me. I have health issues that I cannot work on. What keeps me busy right now? I believe the Lord wanted me to take care of my husband. I was not really a wife. He was taking care of me more. God has a season for me to take care of my house. God wanted to place things in order. Give my time to the Lord. I joined the Zoom group and spent time praying.

What Words of Wisdom do you Want to Impart to the Nurses?

For the Nurses who are coming here to America, make sure you love taking care of people. Especially these days, it is more challenging now than before because all things are computerized. Everything is a computer, and at times, you overlook the patient. That is why in informatics, we did it so you have more time for the patient. Be sure you love taking care of people, and the money will come.

Do not overwork. Take care of your body. This is the temple of the spirit. Leave everything to the lord for your life. No matter what happens to you, God will take care of you. Sometimes you don't know if it still is nursing.

CHAPTER ELEVEN

NEVER GIVE UP ON YOUR DREAM OF BECOMING A NURSE

ALICE B.

Zamboanga City

Early Days

I grew up one hour away from the city. I was in my third year of high school when we had electricity. I would use a candle to study my lessons. We were eight siblings, and I was the youngest of eight. Life was hard growing up. It was a struggle. My parents had no permanent jobs, but they owned land and did farming to support us.

I remember we have to walk to go school. After my elementary years, high school was farther. We have to walk for one hour in the morning to go to school and one hour to go back. The struggles paid off, and despite the struggles, I graduated valedictorian in elementary and high school.

I wanted to be a nurse after high school, but we could not afford the tuition and the books. I ended up taking a Bachelor of Science in Education. I was a teacher.

Life After Graduation

I could not find work, and I knew I needed to help my family. I applied as a nanny in Saudi Arabia. I was told that my salary would be 600 dollars a month. When I started working, the agency gave me 40 dollars a month. This was in the early 2000s. The family that I worked for was kind enough to provide me with about 100 dollars a month. I took care of 4 children and stayed with them for five years. I went back to the Philippines and was able to work as a teacher.

I worked as a government teacher for three years. I later resigned so I could take care of my niece, whose parents were in the US. After she left for the US, I went to Manila and enrolled as a caregiver in one of the schools. Later, I became a teacher at this school.

Coming To America

I came to America via a fiancée visa. I ended up in Pennsylvania. While in Pennsylvania, I worked as a Certified Nursing Assistant for a couple of years. The work was hard. It was physical work. I then enrolled for the License Practical Nurse(LPN).This was a shorter course of study to be a nurse. As an LPN, we have a limited scope of practice. There are things that we cannot do compared to the registered nurses. The work was as physically demanding.

Becoming a Registered Nurse

In 2013, my husband and I decided to adopt a child. I have to be in the Philippines for two years to make this happen. While waiting for the adoption, I decided to go to school to be a registered nurse. I enrolled at Western Mindanao State University. I remember as I was going again to the school campus that it was 30 years ago that I wanted to be a nurse, and here I am after 30 years of becoming one.

I finished school and took the licensing in the Philippines. I have to be a Philippines board passer before I will be able to take the NCLEX.

Working As A Nurse in America

I worked first as an LPN in a nursing home and later worked in a doctor's office. As an LPN in the nursing home, I have to be on my feet, making sure that all the medications are given, and patients are being taken care of. I transitioned to working in a doctor's office. Life working in a small doctor's office is different. The benefits are different. I later decided to work in the prison system as an LPN since I did not take the board exam yet, and later after passing the NCLEX, I worked as a registered nurse. The challenges of working in the prison system are different, but the benefits are great. One of the things that you have to get used to is the name-calling that inmates make when one has to pass medications. I hear catcalls and other stuff. Now, I do more supervisory kind of work. I don't deal with the name-calling anymore.

Working As a Nurse During Covid

The hardest part of working during COVID is the fear that I will bring the illness to my family. We have call-offs from the staff who got sick, so we have to pick up shifts so we can take care of our people. We have to gown up and cover ourselves to see patients. I worked so much overtime that I felt so tired when I got home.

Words of Wisdom

Never give up on your dreams. It might take years to come. It might take different paths, but it will surely come. Always do the right thing even though no one sees it. Above all, keep that faith and always pray that God will guide you in the decisions that you will make.

CHAPTER TWELVE

I DID NOT WANT TO COME USA. I'M GLAD I DID

YOLLIE J.
Manila

Growing years.

My name is Yollie, and I grew up in Olongapo City. My dad worked in the Subic Naval base. That is where I grew up. I grew up with all the influences of American tradition because of where my dad was working. It was an American base. My dad came to America ahead of us in 1993 when the Subic base closed. He was given the opportunity to come here because of his work.

School days

I went to Far Eastern University. In Elementary I went to school in my place, and in High School I went to St Joseph High School. I graduated in 1989 with a degree in Nursing,

Why did you become a Nurse?

I studied to become a nurse. I remember I was five years old when my grandma became sick. I took care of her, and I continued my passion. I did not want to come to America. I was very patriotic. All the nurses were coming to America, and I wanted to stay in the Philippines. So my family, dad, brothers, and mom all came to America. Their point of entry was in Hawaii. I left out because I was overaged. I was 24 at that time. I cannot go here, but at that time, I really did not want to come. I also had a boyfriend at that time.

I got married, and after my second child, My dad told me to give opportunities to my children that are not available in the Philippines. He said, "You and your husband, your future is set, and your husband. How about your children? You have the chance to give them an opportunity to live in another country, don't deny them that ." So I said ok, and I talked to my husband. Financially we were ok. We didn't have to come here. He was working as an Engineer.

Graduation and Work after Nursing School

I was 20 when I graduated from Nursing school. We were in the mall, and my friends and someone told us that there was an opening in Makati Med. So we were wearing our shirts and went to Makati, and we said we wanted to apply as a nurse. The HR (Human Resources) looked at us and said do you want to work here? In that hospital, I worked in ICU (Intensive Care Unit) and stayed for 12 years.

Coming to America

I thought about what my dad said, and I applied. In the middle of my application, I got pregnant again. My second girl was almost a year old at that time. We got approved to go for the interview. We were to go for the visa interview, and 911 happened, so we got pushed back for a year. I thought I was going to give birth to my son in America.

I came to America in August of 2001. I had a choice, and I was waiting for my dad's petition. I could have just waited for my dad's petition, but I said I really needed to understand what nursing is in the USA. So I passed the CGFNS (Commission on Graduate of Foreign Nursing School), TOEFL(Test of English as a Foreign Language), and TSE (Test for Spoken English).

58

When I came to America, I took it under the Texas board, but I took it in Hawaii. I have to pass the CGFNS, TOEFL, TSE, and

Medical exams. Once you pass all of these, then you can go to America. I still needed to take NCLEX at that time. There was no NCLEX in the Philippines. You have to take it here in America. I waited for two months in Hawaii and took it under the Texas board.

Destination in America

I went to Victoria, Texas, and came under contract with an agency. After a year, the hospital brought our contract. I asked the hospital later if we had a contract with them, and they said that we didn't have a contract with them. I think they want us out of the agency so they can pay us directly. We stayed here for two years, and we came to Arizona.

First Time Working in an American Hospital

It was really not a hard transition because, in Makati Med in the CVICU, they taught us the American standard. We were charting the American standard way. When I came to America, they gave me 90 days of training and released after to work independently.

Struggles working in an American Hospital

When I first started working here, my struggle was understanding how they talk. It is not that we don't understand English. We speak and know about it, but listening to them is different. I remember there was this doctor who said, "Yollie, I am admitting this patient." All I heard was blahhh blahhh. I did not know what to write in the order. So I asked my charge nurse. She knew my struggles in trying to understand the doctors, so my charge nurse told me to call him back and ask him to speak slowly. So, I did. He said, "Oh I'm sorry you are not used to it." He gave me the orders for the patient.

After that, I watched a lot of TV and movies. I talked back to the TV, and after that, I was fine.

Career Ladder

I was a regular staff nurse in the ICU. Always been an ICU nurse and PACU nurse. After five years of being a staff nurse, they wanted me to train as a charge nurse. I refused. I did not want to be responsible for the unit when I didn't understand the unit myself. After five years, though, they don't have an open position. They opened one officially, so I can work as the charge.

I am a Clinical Coordinator now. I work the day shift, so I manage the unit for one of the heart hospitals here in Arizona. As a Clinical Coordinator, I manage the unit, the staff, and the schedule. A clinical coordinator is a unit manager who manages the doctors, staff, and complaints. Sometimes I do bedside work.

Struggles In America

My family grew up here I really did not have a struggle. My eldest was three years old when she came here. Basically, they don't know any other life.

My husband stopped working to take care of the kids. He worked part-time, but then he got Valley Fever, so I told him not to work outside anymore.

Words of Wisdom

Coming here, you have to have experience. Get an experience in your belt. Nursing in America is a different kind of nursing. The pace is faster. They come as a new nurse. Some would quit, and some of them become successful.

It would help if you also have a support system. You have to have friends who can support you. If you have family or kids, you have to connect with people to understand you. Some would, some not. But we have a lot who take care of other nurses. That is why you have to join organizations such as the Philippines Nurse of Arizona. We take care of you.

My children are nurses. I did not want to be nurses, but they wanted to be nurses. Two of them are nurses. They want to take care of people.

CHAPTER THIRTEEN
CALLED TO BE A NURSE

MARICRIS T.

Pampanga

Early years

I was born in Angeles City, a city in Pampanga. My parents were Mario and Ester. I have three siblings, and I am the only girl in the family. I went to preschool and high school at Holy Spirit Family Academy and Angeles University for College. I took my Masters here in the United States at Aspen University.

What Made You Take Nursing?

It is really a funny story. You know, in high school, they make you take a test. They do an assessment. I guess I scored high in nursing, so I took nursing. Also, during that time, everyone was taking up nursing, so I guess I went ahead and took nursing, so that was what I did.

After College Graduation

I graduated from nursing in 1992. After graduation, I volunteered at the local hospital in my city and eventually got hired there. This is a government facility or hospital. Working here was the foundation of my nursing career. So I worked in this hospital for nine years before coming to America.

How Did You Come To America?

I applied at IPAMS (recruitment agency). This is an agency in the Philippines that takes nurses to come here to the United States. I went to the USA in 2001, so it was roughly after nine years after I graduated in Nursing. I was recruited to work in Victoria, Texas. This was where I initially came when I first came to the USA.

What Were Your Struggles When You First Worked In the US?

My struggle when I first came was this. I was an OR (operating room) nurse in my country. Then when I came here, I had to be floated to the Telemetry Unit (a unit where cardiac monitoring is needed.).We never had that unit in my country. So I literally had to learn and relearn. I tried to learn everything. After three months of being in this unit, they trained me to be a charge nurse.

First Time Working in The Hospital

I was kind of scared. You know I came from a government hospital in my country. You use a thermometer where you shake it and then use it. When I went to Texas, the unit had machines that take all your vital signs. I have to ask a nurse to show me how to use it.

Career Ladder

I am currently the Director of one of the heart hospitals here. I handle the Cardiovascular unit, Intensive care unit, Step down unit, Nursing admin, and Emergency unit.

I started in the Telemetry unit in Victoria, Texas, until I came here to AZ. I was a Telemetry nurse first. I am the Director now for one of the heart hospitals.

Words of Wisdom

Do it! Coming to the US might be difficult at first, but with a lot of hard work and if you will try, it will be good. Filipino nurses are one of the best nurses. I see their capabilities all the time.

CHAPTER FOURTEEN

HOME CARE OWNER

ELIZABETH V.
Zamboanga City

Tell Us About Your Growing Years

About my childhood, I have a typical normal Filipino childhood. We were told to do household chores, like washing dishes, cooking, and cleaning the house. We were allowed to play outside the house with my friends around the neighborhood. I really don't think that my childhood is hard. My mom was a government employee, and my father worked as a jeepney operator. I went to a public school, a university school that also has elementary to high school students. I remember going to school. We have to walk 20 to 30 minutes each way to reach the school. These experiences molded me into who I am today.

What Made You Take Up Nursing

Taking up Nursing has been my ambition since I was in grade school. I remember the sister of my father was a nurse at that time, and I really looked up to her. Because of her, I was inspired to take up nursing .Going to America was not part of it when I was young. I did not know that you could come to America to be a nurse. All I wanted was to see myself wearing the all-white nursing uniform.

What Were Your Struggles During Nursing School

Being in nursing school was not easy at all. I needed to study harder if I wanted to pass every subject. Aside from this, there were also the financial obligations that my parents needed to do. There are no student loans that I know that we can borrow when going to school.

Even though my parents had jobs, I knew they needed to work double time or look for other means to sustain my tuition. I am forever grateful for all the support they gave me.

Life After Nursing Graduation

After graduation, I have to review right away for my board examination. After passing my board examination, I was so excited to work. However, the nursing job in the Philippines, work-wise, was not great. There was no work. I have to apply as a volunteer nurse in a private hospital. After a couple of years working in a private hospital, I was hired to work in a government hospital, which offers a more stable job and a better salary.

What Were The Steps You Did To Come To America

The hiring of nurses in the USA was really in demand. I was referred to an agency. I needed to take CGFNS, IELTS, and NCLEX as the requirements to get the immigrant visa to come to the USA as a nurse.

My application was filed in 2006. Unfortunately, the recession was starting to hit the US, and they stopped granting visas to nurses. So I thought that it was not my time yet to come to the USA. I believe God has a better plan for me. I was not expecting my application will push through. In 2012, the USA started granting visas for nursing again. I thought that my application was not on file anymore, but when I checked online, my status was already current. So I guess this is God's perfect time for me to go with my American dream.

There were hurdles that I needed to do before I came to the USA. All my visa requirements were expired. So I have to take my IELTS and my TOEFL all over again. I have to prepare myself financially to take the tests. The test was given on another island. So I have to travel to another Island to take the test. All the traveling costs more money.

When Did You Come to America

I came to America in 2015. It is a new beginning for here in America. I was so amazed by the place. I will be speaking English every day, hahaha (laughing). Everything is different in America.

Your First Time Working in America

I was slightly nervous when I first started my first job in America. The big adjustment was communication. I know how to speak English, but hearing different accents from different people was really my big adjustment, especially when you have to deal with doctors. That was the beginning, but as you get along the way, I learned how to adjust and get used to it.

What Were Your Initial Struggles?

The nursing job here is not easy. It is physically, mentally, and psychologically a challenging calling. I was dealing with different people from different cultures. I have to deal with my patients as well. At one point, I asked myself, what am I doing here? I was thinking that in the Philippines, my job as a nurse was because I worked in an outpatient setting. I don't have to clean the behind of other people that I don't know. I love my patients, though, and it becomes easier if you have that love. I am constantly learning every time I come to work.

Tell us About The Pandemic. Your Thoughts and Struggles

Everybody was afraid of Covid. No one wants to get sick because of Covid. I feel that the media exaggerates the issue, but the nurses don't have a choice. I have to go to work. I made sure I had to protect myself first. It was really difficult working with all the protection gear. It was not fun, but that was the only protection we had at that time until the vaccines came. During this pandemic, my parents in the Philippines got sick with Covid. I was so downhearted here because I could not be with them. I thank my God because He never left me and my parents during this time. The Lord gave me the strength. I needed to work overtime to support my parents' needs when they were both admitted to the hospital because of Covid. That was the lowest point in my life.

Your Career Ladder

Presently, I have given up working at the bedside as a nurse. My husband, who is also a nurse, and I decided to run our own business, a group home for disabled people.

Wisdom You Want To Share To The Nurses Who are Here in America and Those Who Are Planning to Come

Being a nurse is not just a job. You need to love it. You must have the compassion to do it. You must embrace all the trials that come your way because you will learn from them. As one of my patients said, "I don't know how you guys do this kind of job." Patients inspire us nurses to make our duties more meaningful. But above all, I thank God for everything, for all the blessings He gave us.

To those nurses who plan to do their American dream, pray to God for his guidance and wisdom. When you finally come, that is the perfect time given to you. It is not easy, but it is worth it.

CHAPTER FIFTEEN

A DREAM AND PERSEVERANCE

MARY

Gapan City

I have been in the US since early 2000. I am from the Philippines in a town called Gapan. I have another brother. He is also a nurse and is currently working in London. Nursing runs in the family. I have another cousin who is a nurse.

My mom and dad were both teachers. They are both elementary school teachers. My mom was a first-grade teacher, and my dad retired as a supervisor.

My educational background. I started when I was three, as my nanny could not care for me anymore. I was going with my mom to school. The school was just in front of our house. As early as three years old, I was in school. In high school, I went to a Catholic school.

Why Nursing

I had to choose between taking up nursing or becoming a teacher. I did not want to become a teacher, so I decided to be a nurse. I graduated in 1997 from a college in Cabanatuan City. Back then, there were few people taking up nursing because no one was hiring to come to the US. I think there were only 30 people who graduated in the year for that class.

Life After College Graduation

I was able to work as a nurse in one of the government hospitals in our place in Cabanatuan. It was hard to get work, so I started as a volunteer nurse for six months. I worked without pay. I worked in well

70

baby, Neonatal Intensive Care Unit. I worked in every area of the hospital. I worked in this hospital for a year or two.

I decided to come to the US via a tourist visa and luckily I was granted a multiple entry as a tourist.

Journey as a US RN

When I finally came to the US. I challenged the board so I could take the NCLEX. We were able to do this before, and luckily, I passed. Back then, it was before 9/11. It was easier. I stayed with my cousin for a while because I lacked resources. I told myself I was already here, and I did not want to go back home. I'll see what is in store for me.

I did not take the CGFNS. I took the NCLEX. I did not take the TOEFL, but I took the Michigan test. Those are just requirements. You have to pass the California board, Michigan test and submit those to CGFNS.

Looking for the Nursing Job

I went to the hospitals around the area where my cousin lives. I went from one hospital to another, but no one wanted to hire me until I finally found a hospital willing to sponsor me in Southern California. I was in San Jose first. I went to Los Angeles just to get the paperwork.

Once you get hired, the process at that time was for you to do all the paperwork. They will sponsor you, but you will have to do all the paperwork. I worked and processed then immigration paperwork from social security. You have to fall in line just to get social security. I remember I was in the line at 10 o'clock in the evening and did not get finished until the next day. So here, I was able to get the work permit and social security. I did not know anybody in LA. I was just a person with a dream.

The hospital that sponsored me gave me six months of housing. Since I was in contract, they paid me so low. At that time, they paid me about $16. So I worked nights and rented a room to one of the co-workers working in the hospital.

I started working in surgery, and I told them I could not because of the on-call. I do not have a car. I just ride a bus. I did not even know how to ride a bus. I have to ride two rides. The distance where I lived was only about 10 miles away from my workplace, but you need two bus rides to get to my work. If you miss the first bus, then you miss the second bus. Early in the morning, after work, you want to go home, but you have to take two buses to go home. I did this for two months and said that I needed to buy a car.

Working as a Nurse Finally

There were not many struggles. I can adapt easily. I started in the surgery department, and then I went to Med – Surg(Medical Surgical unit). It was different in a hospital setting. So, of course, now you have the machine, and you have doctors looking for you. I adjusted easily because I wanted to prove to my mom and dad that I could make it. I was the typical Filipino, I would share and give my family what I had, but they didn't ask for anything. My parents know how to live simply and are contented.

It took me three years after I came to America before I was able to go home to the Philippines. I finished my three years contract with the hospital and went home.

Life Struggles In America You don't have any family. It was hard. You are by yourself. I had a family, my cousin, who was far from me in Northern California.

I was by myself in Southern California. I have to survive. The hospital where I worked had a lot of Filipinos. I was the youngest back then, so they treated me as their youngest. They were all the "ates." (older sisters)

The holidays were a struggle because you were by yourself (our eyes were tearing up as if we were brought back to that time). I just worked every holiday.

Finding The State To Live

I finally moved to Arizona in 2006. The reason why we moved here was because of my son. My doctor said we had to move over to the desert because my son had an Asthma attack every two months. So we are here. My cousin later moved here. So now I have a family.

During Covid

It was a difficult time. I was among the first ones in the hospital to have Covid. I was the very first one. It was difficult because of isolation. My kids were still small back then, so I looked at them through face time. Even if I see them through face time, it is not easy because you cannot hug them. The isolation was difficult at that time; you cannot get out of isolation until you have a negative test. I was in isolation for more than a month, at least eight weeks.

Work during Covid was not very difficult as I was working in the clinic. PPE (Personal Protective Equipment) was provided.

Career Ladder

I graduated with my BSN. I started in Med-Surg. Then as a part-time house supervisor, clinical coordinator, and later worked in an outpatient setting in one of the hospitals as the team leader.

Words of Wisdom

It is a good opportunity for those thinking about coming to America. It is tough initially. Just think about the future. For the nurses who are working, life is short. After Covid, you realize things and those material things are not as important. Spend time with family, love everybody around you, and share your love.

CHAPTER SIXTEEN

HERE WE ARE

A young Emily, growing up in the Philippines.

Nursing is a great profession to be in. It is a field that allows you to wear many different hats without having to leave the profession. If you get worn out from doing bedside nursing, there's teaching, research, clinical adjunct, informatics, etc. While nursing pays good, it is hard work. Expect and be prepared to work hard. -Emily

When adversities and challenges come your way, keep going and believe that when you think it is over, God will send you miracles. -Rizza

The moment the American dream was fulfilled. A pose at the airport once the plane landed in America. –Paulo

In coming to America, you need a lot of courage. When you start in America, you start good as zero. I realized after graduation that success can be achieved from the strategies that you do in life.-Paulo

Do not overwork. Take care of your body. This is the temple of the spirit. Leave everything to the lord for your life. No matter what happens to you, God will take care of you. Sometimes
you don't know if it still is nursing.-Maine

Being a Nurse is not just a job. You need to love it. You must have the compassion to do it. You must embrace all the trials that come your way because you will learn from them, as one of my patients said. "I don't know how you guys do this kind of job."

Patients inspire us nurses to make our duties more meaningful.- Elizabeth

You also need to have support. You have to have friends who can support you. If you have family or kids, you have to connect with people to understand you. –Yollie

Enjoy life do not dwell some sentiments. Whatever you can help to others do it. Sometimes there would be regrets if you won't be able to help. -Emma

Do it! Coming to the US might be difficult at first, but with a lot of hard work and if you try, it will be good. Filipino nurses are one of the best nurses.-Maricris

You have to love what you are doing. It has to come from the heart. When I won the Daisy Award (recognition given to the superhuman- work nurses do), I never thought I would get it.

Never stop dreaming and aiming for a better life. Nursing is a very noble job where you make a difference in people's lives. – Sonia

Taken during our second year in college for the Pinning Ceremony. The ceremony symbolizes our transition into the nursing profession. The author with her classmates during the Pinning Ceremony.

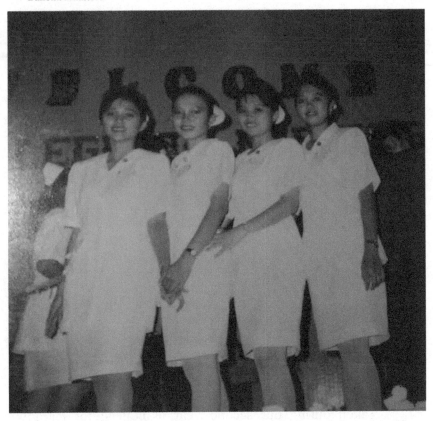

Graduation time. The beginning of that wonderful journey of being a nurse. Author second from left - Minnerva

Trying to teach my children where I came from by exposing them to activities such as this one. Here with the bahay kubo (nipa hut) background. - Minnerva

CHAPTER SEVENTEEN

IN MEMORY

Remembering our fellow nurses who lost their lives during COVID while trying to save others.

We honor them today, and we remember them not as part of the statistics but as someone who touched many people's lives, including ours. Let us have a moment of silence and pray for the families and friends they left behind.

Record my misery; list my tears on your scroll- Are they not in your record? Psalm 56:8

Acknowledgement

Making this book to showcase our Filipino nurses has been a dream that took a long time to fulfill. This dream was born as I was talking to one of the nurses who shared her story on her journey to come to America. Her story of struggle and triumph inspired me, and I thought there must be hundreds out there that I could tell their story and inspire others. I then met Charity Norman, to whom I am indebted. She showed me the ropes on how to start this project. Without her guidance, I will still be in the dreaming phase. Thank you, Charity.

To our nurses who shared their stories, I would like to let you know that your stories touched me in a way that I remember the tears I shed as we talked, the strength in knowing that setbacks are just but temporary, and above all, I am reminded that there are no obstacles in the world that can hinder a determined person from fulfilling their dreams.

To my dearest family, who have been my strength, thank you for what you do to ensure that I have the time to do this writing. May you be inspired in knowing that even though mom is past the prime age, dreams can still be fulfilled. For with God, nothing is impossible.

About The Author

Binibini Minnerva is a Nurse Practitioner. She started her nursing career as a registered nurse. She furthered her studies after coming to America and, in 2007, graduated with a degree in Family Nurse Practitioner. In 2019, she earned her Doctor in Nursing Practice degree. She has more than 20 years of experience as a nurse. She is currently working in the hospital as a Nurse Practitioner. Her passion for seeing our nurses grow and flourish in their chosen profession compelled her to be an active officer for the local Filipino nursing organization. Her vision to make sure that the new generation will love nursing is evident as she also works as an adjunct faculty in one of the colleges. Binibini Minnerva currently lives in Arizona with her husband and two children. One of her children is following in his mom's footsteps and is taking up nursing.